Exploring Android 15

Innovations, Enhancements, and the

Future of the Platform

David Wilson

Table of contents

Exploring Android 15

Introduction

The most recent version of Google's mobile operating system, known as Android 15, is expected to offer a slew of new features, improvements, and optimizations to Android-powered gadgets. Google strives to enhance security, boost performance, improve user experience, and add cutting-edge features that meet the changing needs of both users and developers with every new release. This article explores the fascinating world of Android 15, including its timeline, supported devices, visual updates, features, improved user experience, technical advancements, developer insights, and a prediction for the ecosystem's future.

With Android powering billions of smartphones, tablets, wearables, and other connected devices globally, the platform has come to be associated with creativity and adaptability. Ever since its establishment, Google has been dedicated to expanding the potential of the Android platform, supporting a thriving community of applications and services, and providing a smooth and easy-to-use interface across a variety of hardware setups. Google is carrying on this history of excellence with Android 15, expanding on the work of its forebears and pushing the limits of what is feasible in the mobile realm.

Android's open-source nature, which enables developers to make custom ROMs, alter system behaviors, and contribute to the platform's continued development, is one of its distinguishing features. Android 15 upholds this open-minded philosophy while bringing a ton of new features and improvements aimed at boosting user happiness, productivity, and privacy. Android 15 contains features that will appeal to all types of smartphone users, including power users, seasoned developers, and casual users.

We'll go into all aspects of Android 15 in this post, beginning with a synopsis of its release schedule and compatible devices. After that, we'll examine the naming conventions and visual upgrades that Google used for this release. After that, we'll take a close look at the enhancements and new features included in Android 15. We'll discuss everything, including updates to the privacy sandbox, virtual MIDI 2.0 compatibility, camera upgrades, and screen sharing advances.

We'll then focus on the improvements to the user experience that Android 15 brought about, such as the return of lock screen widgets, support for app pairings, an easy mode for new users, and the addition of a private space feature for increased security and privacy. We'll also look at the internal technological upgrades, such support for Bluetooth LE audio, performance increases, and improvements to file integrity.

Android 15 offers a plethora of new tools, APIs, and platform improvements for developers with the goal of optimizing performance, enhancing app development efficiency, and extending the functionality of Android apps. Our coverage will include the Android 15 developer preview, tools for testing and development, updates to the API, and additions. Developers can anticipate insightful information about this version and how to exploit its capabilities to craft engaging user experiences.

To sum up, Android 15 is a significant release that marks another turning point in the development of Google's mobile platform. It comes with a plethora of new features, improvements, and optimizations that aim to completely transform the

Android experience for both consumers and developers. Looking ahead, Android looks to have a stronger future than it has ever had because to ongoing innovation, teamwork, and community involvement. With its impressive balance of power, flexibility, and simplicity, Android 15 is sure to impress both longstanding Android enthusiasts and those who are new to the ecosystem.

Chapter 1: Overview of Android 15

An important turning point in the development of the Android platform is represented by Android 15, the most recent version of Google's mobile operating system. Android 15 seeks to raise the bar for mobile computing by emphasizing performance, user experience, and new feature introduction. We will outline the Android 15 release schedule as well as the compatible devices that will get the update in this part.

Schedule of Release

For significant Android updates, such as Android 15, Google adheres to a set delivery schedule. Beginning with developer previews and ending with the public stable release, this timetable usually consists of multiple phases. The Android 15 release schedule is broken out as follows:

1. Developer Sneak Peaks: Early developer previews of Android 15 are made available by Google to give developers access to new features and APIs. With the help of these previews, developers can verify that their apps work properly on the new platform by testing them. It is common practice to issue developer previews in numerous iterations,

each of which adds new features and improvements.

2. Releases in beta: Google delivers Android 15 beta versions to a broader audience, comprising enthusiasts and early adopters, after the developer previews. A wider number of users are meant to test beta releases, which are more stable than developer previews. Google uses feedback from beta testers to find and fix bugs and performance problems prior to the final release.

3. Consistent Release: Google releases the stable version of Android 15 to compatible devices after the beta testing process is over and any necessary adjustments have been made. The stable release, which comes with

all the features and optimizations added during the preview and beta stages, is the version of Android 15 that is advised for widespread consumer use.

Accommodated Devices

Depending on the brand and type of the device, Android 15 is not always available. Android upgrades are usually released to Google Pixel handsets first, then to other manufacturers' devices. Below is a summary of the Android 15 compatible devices:

Among the first to receive Android 15 updates are the Google Pixel Series devices, which include the Pixel 8, Pixel 8 Pro, Pixel 7a, Pixel 7, Pixel 7 Pro, Pixel 6a, Pixel 6,

Pixel 6 Pro, Pixel Fold, and Pixel Tablet. In order to give customers a consistent and modern experience, Google continues to deliver security fixes and full OS updates for Pixel devices for several years after they are first released.

Additional Android Devices: Other Android smartphones and tablets from different manufacturers might possibly get updates to Android 15 in addition to Pixel devices. The age of the device, the hardware specs, and the update policies of the manufacturer are some of the elements that determine whether or not updates are available for non-Pixel devices. Updates for flagship and mid-range devices are usually available from manufacturers like Samsung, OnePlus,

Asus, and Motorola, however availability and time can differ.

All things considered, the Android 15 release schedule and list of compatible devices show Google's dedication to providing regular upgrades and guaranteeing a unified user experience across a variety of platforms.

Google lets users and developers engage in testing and improvement through early access to developer previews and beta releases, which eventually results in a more polished and feature-rich final release. Users may anticipate experiencing the newest features, improvements, and optimizations that Android 15 has to offer as it becomes available for compatible devices.

Chapter 2: Visual Updates and Name

Name and Version Information

Android versions are usually titled after sweet delicacies or desserts in alphabetical order. This also applies to the future Android operating system version, Android 15. Google has decided to name Android 15 "Vanilla Ice Cream," which is a fun homage to their practice of naming each version after a delicious treat. Android version names are arranged alphabetically, which makes it simple for users to predict when new releases will be available and adds some amusement to the software updating procedure.

Android 15 is distinguished not only by its name but also by its version number, which offers vital details on its position within the Android ecosystem. Version numbers make it easier for developers and users to determine the relevance and age of a certain release. As an illustration, Android 15 represents a substantial update to the Android range, probably bringing with it a host of new features, enhancements, and optimizations over its forerunners.

Google's versioning strategy for Android guarantees coherence and consistency throughout the program's development. Google keeps the Android ecosystem cohesive and orderly by adhering to a set name convention and numbering scheme, which promotes understanding and communication among users, developers, and other stakeholders.

Interesting Looks

With the goal of enhancing both the operating system's overall aesthetic appeal and user experience, Android 15 brings a number of visual improvements. These improvements cover all facets of the user interface, such as the overall design language, logos, and icons.

The new Android 15 logo is one prominent visual improvement. The triangle-shaped logo, which has a green outline, displays the well-known bugdroid mascot, which has a "15" on its back. With the logo set against a starry sky, Android's concept of innovation and technological growth is echoed with a feeling of futurism and exploration.

In addition, Android 15 keeps its space-themed visual identity, expanding on the design language introduced in earlier versions. The addition of space-themed components serves to further emphasize Android's reputation as a platform that pushes limits and discovers uncharted territory.

The entire user interface, including the font and iconography, has been subtly altered in Android 15, in addition to the logo. With these improvements, users should be guaranteed a uniform and aesthetically pleasant experience throughout the operating system in terms of readability, accessibility, and coherence.

All things considered, Google's dedication to design brilliance and user-centric innovation is carried through in the aesthetic enhancements of Android 15. Android wants to give customers a great and immersive experience that embodies the platform's forward-thinking values through constant improvement and evolution of its visual language.

Chapter 3: Features and Upgrades

Improving Screen Sharing

With Android 15, screen sharing is significantly improved, giving users more privacy and control over screen captures. Partial screen sharing is a noteworthy enhancement that lets users record only certain programs while concealing notifications and other private data from view.

With the ability to record only the content they choose to share and conceal other notifications and apps, users can finally allay privacy concerns related to screen recording. Android 15 enables users to take excellent recordings without sacrificing their security or privacy by providing them with fine-grained control over screen sharing.

In addition, Pixel smartphones will be the first to get this feature through Android 14 QPR2, which will be released as the March Pixel Feature Drop. In order to give consumers access to the newest features and upgrades as soon as they become available, Google has demonstrated its commitment to rapid updates and improvements for its flagship products.

Overall, Android 15's screen sharing improvements make it safer and easier for users to share their displays without disclosing private information, which is a major step forward for user privacy and control.

Revisions to the Camera

Android 15 brings a number of improvements targeted at enhancing smartphone cameras' usefulness and performance. Enhancements for low-light photography, sophisticated flash strength settings, and optimizations for third-party camera apps are some of these changes.

One significant advancement is the capacity for developers to increase the camera's viewfinder's brightness in dim light, giving consumers greater sight and clarity when taking pictures or recording videos in difficult lighting circumstances. For customers who utilize third-party camera apps for photography and filming, this improvement is very helpful.

Furthermore, the enhanced flash strength adjustments in Android 15 enable developers to precisely modify the flash's intensity according to user preferences and lighting circumstances. Its adaptability lets users use the flash to its full potential in a variety of shooting situations, improving the overall quality of their images and movies.

Ultimately, Android 15's camera upgrades are meant to improve user experience and let people take better smartphone images and movies. Android 15 encourages users to express themselves creatively through photography and videography by giving developers the access and tools they need to maximize camera performance.

Upgrading to Virtual MIDI 2.0

With the addition of virtual MIDI 2.0 device support, Android 15 expands the platform's potential for musicians and music lovers. This feature expands on earlier improvements made in Android 13, such as the addition of MIDI 2.0 USB device support.

Android 15 offers new opportunities for music creation and performance on the platform by supporting virtual MIDI 2.0, which enables composition applications to operate synthesizer apps as virtual MIDI 2.0 devices.

By utilizing this feature, musicians may easily incorporate their preferred synthesis and composition tools, resulting in rich and expressive musical experiences on their Android smartphones.

Moreover, Google's sustained investment in MIDI technology highlights the platform's dedication to promoting artistic pursuits and innovation within the music business. Android 15 opens up new possibilities for artistic expression and collaboration by giving developers access to powerful MIDI capabilities, enabling artists to push the limits of what's possible on mobile devices.

All things considered, the platform's music ecosystem has reached a major turning point with the addition of virtual MIDI 2.0 support in Android 15, making it more appealing to producers, musicians, and music lovers.

Updates to the Privacy Sandbox

With Android 15, Google's effort to improve user security and privacy across all of its operating systems, the Privacy Sandbox, receives upgrades. These changes are intended to provide consumers greater choice over their online privacy and data, all the while maintaining the ability to offer relevant and targeted ads in a way that respects their right to privacy.

Elevating Android AD Services to extension level 10 is a significant improvement that enables it to integrate the most recent Privacy Sandbox modifications. Thanks to this improvement, Android 15 can now provide users with even more sophisticated privacy measures and safeguards, guaranteeing that their personal data is protected from misuse or illegal access.

Furthermore, new Health Connect data types are integrated into Android 15, enabling standardized health data sharing and storage across Android apps. With this feature, users can keep control over their private health information and enjoy the benefits of seamless integration with health-related apps and services, all while improving privacy and security in the healthcare arena.

All things considered, Google's efforts to give user privacy and security first priority have advanced significantly with the Privacy Sandbox updates in Android 15. With Android 15, users can enjoy a more secure and safe digital experience without compromising the ease of use and functionality of their smartphones thanks to the addition of new privacy features and enhancements.

Chapter 4: Improvements to User Experience

Screen Lock Widgets

With the probable reintroduction of lock screen widgets, a feature that was available in previous Android versions but was progressively taken out, Android 15 adds a nostalgic touch to the user experience. A "communal space" feature that was added to an Android 14 release that is still in development raises the possibility that Android 15 will bring back lock screen widgets, giving users a programmable area on their lock screens for instant access to data and app features.

Though it's still in its early stages of development, the lock screen widgets feature provides a glimpse into the possibility of a comeback for this useful feature.

Anticipate a space on the lock screen where users can install compatible widgets to provide quick access to information without having to unlock the smartphone. This feature could improve accessibility and customizing possibilities for several people sharing a device, and it could be especially helpful on tablets and multi-user devices.

Although the implementation details are still concealed by flags and are still being worked on, the possibility of lock screen widgets making a comeback in Android 15 is a sign of Google's dedication to giving users a more effective and personalized UI that can accommodate a range of user requirements and preferences.

App Pairs

Android 15, which may provide the option to save and retrieve app pairs straight from the home screen, is an attempt to improve multitasking capabilities in light of the growing popularity of larger Android phones and foldable devices. The increased tendency toward larger displays and the desire for better multitasking on contemporary smartphones are the reasons behind this feature's creation.

App pairing is the idea of grouping two compatible apps together so that users can tap once to activate both of them at once. Although some manufacturers have previously included comparable functionalities on their foldable devices, Google's addition of app pairings to Android 15 may offer a more uniform and efficient method for achieving this capability.

Given that users of foldable smartphones, such as the Google Pixel Fold, are more inclined to multitask, this improvement is especially pertinent. Users will find it easier to navigate between their favorite app combinations and more efficient if they can save and immediately retrieve app pairs from the home screen.

Android 15's possible support for app pairs shows a dedication to improving the user experience for a variety of hardware configurations, promoting a more fluid and user-friendly interface with the operating system by taking into account the changing form factors of Android devices.

Simple Mode

As smartphones develop further into strong, feature-rich gadgets, not everyone is equally at ease or skilled at utilizing the intricacies of contemporary technology. In order to accommodate customers who might find some parts of using a smartphone difficult, Android 15 may provide a "easy pre-set" option in response to this worry.

The Android 14 QPR3 beta's "easy pre-set" mode is a sign of a feature that will simplify the UI and make it more approachable for a wider range of users. It is anticipated that this mode will remove wallpapers, boost contrast, enlarge icons, bold text, and simplify the interface for people who might find it difficult to navigate the complexities of sophisticated smartphone features.

This improvement to the user experience respects the values of accessibility and inclusion by acknowledging that individuals vary in their degree of technological expertise. Android 15 aims to close the gap for customers who might be intimidated by the abundance of functions and options found in modern devices by providing an easy mode.

Even though the easy mode is still in the testing stage and isn't live yet, its inclusion in the beta shows Google's dedication to making Android a platform that can be used by people with different technological backgrounds and tastes.

Secure Area Feature

The "Private Space" feature of Android 15 could be a game-changer for consumers who are worried about the privacy of their critical apps. Similar to a business profile but devoted to safeguarding and separating important apps from the rest of the system, this feature adds an additional profile linked to the primary phone user.

Additional authentication procedures are included in the Private Space feature to guarantee that only authorized users can access the isolated profile. Apps and alerts inside the Private Space are automatically suspended when not in use, providing an additional degree of privacy and security.

The ability to conceal the Private Space and limit access to it to a certain search phrase adds even more discretion to this tool. The additional security protections provided by the Private Space feature can be advantageous to users who are worried about unwanted access to critical applications by others.

This innovation gives Android users more powerful options to protect their personal data, in line with the rising emphasis on user privacy and security. One example of Google's commitment to provide cutting-edge privacy capabilities without sacrificing the ease of use and convenience of the Android platform is the Private Space feature.

Finally, the improvements to the Android 15 user experience highlight Google's dedication to giving consumers a flexible, safe, and adaptable platform. An easier mode, support for app pairings, the possibility of lock screen widgets coming back, and the Private Space feature all help to make Android a more efficient, privacy-aware, and inclusive platform. These improvements demonstrate Google's attentiveness to customer requirements and its continuous endeavors to raise the bar for the Android user experience.

Chapter 5: Technical Enhancements

Updates on File Integrity

Significant improvements to file integrity management are brought to Android 15, strengthening the platform's security and resistance to possible attacks. Among these enhancements include the addition of new APIs that let applications encrypt data using unique cryptographic signatures, guaranteeing that private data is shielded from alteration or unwanted access.

Android 15 has made significant enhancements to file integrity, one of which is the addition of APIs that let apps encrypt data with unique cryptographic signatures. By guaranteeing that files are shielded from unwanted access or alteration, this feature improves data security by lowering the possibility of data breaches or corruption.

Additionally, Android 15 improves the File Integrity Manager by adding new APIs that let apps check the accuracy of files and identify any tampering or unauthorized modifications. By taking a proactive stance when it comes to file integrity management, the danger of malware and other security risks that could try to jeopardize user data or system file integrity is reduced.

All things considered, Android 15's file integrity enhancements mark a major advancement in bolstering the platform's security and resistance to possible attacks. Android 15 enables developers to create more resilient and secure applications that protect user data and privacy by giving them access to powerful tools and APIs for file encryption and integrity verification.

Improvements in Battery Life and Performance

With Android 15, a number of improvements to performance and battery life are made with the goal of maximizing the use of system resources and raising overall device performance. Improved thermal management, a new power-efficiency mode for background tasks, and optimizations for resource-intensive apps like gaming are some of these improvements.

The addition of a power-efficiency mode for background operations, which lets developers tell the system that some jobs don't need a lot of power consumption, is one important improvement. This prolongs the life of device batteries and lessens battery drain by enabling the system to distribute resources more effectively.

Furthermore, by giving developers more direct access to power and thermal systems, Android 15 enhances thermal management. Because of this, developers can eliminate thermal throttling and maximize resource use, guaranteeing steady performance even with high workloads.

Moreover, Android 15 brings enhancements for resource-intensive apps like gaming, enabling developers to better utilize the platform's potential. Smoother performance and increased responsiveness for gaming and multimedia apps are the outcome of these enhancements, which also include improvements to input processing, memory management, and graphics rendering.

All things considered, Android 15's improvements to performance and battery life mark a major advancement in the platform's optimization for greater effectiveness and responsiveness. Android

15 guarantees that consumers can get a more seamless and uniform experience across a broad range of applications and use cases by giving developers tools and improvements for improved resource usage and heat management.

Audio Support for Bluetooth LE

The next-generation Bluetooth LE Audio standard for wireless audio transmission is now supported by Android 15. Compared to conventional Bluetooth audio, this new standard has a number of benefits, such as better audio quality, reduced energy usage, and multi-stream audio transmission capabilities.

The reduced energy consumption of Bluetooth LE Audio is a crucial characteristic that prolongs the battery life of wireless audio equipment like speakers, headphones, and earphones. This improves the overall user experience by enabling consumers to enjoy longer listening sessions without having to constantly recharge their devices.

Because Bluetooth LE Audio makes use of the Low Complexity Communications Codec (LC3), it also enables enhanced audio quality. With reduced latency and greater fidelity audio delivery, this codec offers users a more engaging and entertaining listening experience.

Moreover, Bluetooth LE Audio adds multi-stream audio transmission functionality, enabling users to stream music to several devices at once. This makes it possible for things like seamless audio playback across many rooms in a home audio setup, or audio sharing among multiple users.

All things considered, the addition of Bluetooth LE Audio compatibility to Android 15 marks a noteworthy development in wireless audio technology. Android 15 guarantees that customers will experience better wireless audio quality, longer battery life, and more versatility by using this next-generation standard.

Integrated Phishing Defense

With the addition of integrated phishing protection, Android 15 improves platform security and shields users from dishonest and fraudulent online activity. This feature alerts users to potential hazards by keeping an eye on app activity and looking for indications of phishing or other fraudulent activity.

Google's security framework for Android, Play Protect, is integrated with the built-in phishing prevention in Android 15. In order to provide users with timely alerts and advice on how to protect their devices and personal information, Play Protect keeps an eye on app activity in real-time and analyzes it for indications of phishing or other dangerous conduct.

To supplement the built-in phishing protection, Android 15 also adds additional privacy and security features including improved app permissions and privacy settings. By enabling users to take charge of their digital privacy and security, these features guarantee that users' personal data is kept safe and secure while utilizing Android devices.

Moreover, Android 15 gives developers the information and tools they need to create reliable, safe apps that adhere to security and privacy best practices. Android 15 aims to reduce the risk of phishing and other online risks by fostering a secure app environment, safeguarding users and their personal data.

All things considered, the inclusion of phishing protection by default in Android 15 is a major improvement in mobile security. Through direct integration of this capability into the platform, Android 15 improves the ecosystem's overall security posture and gives users more confidence when using their devices online.

Separating NFC from System Updates

Decoupling NFC (Near Field Communication) components from system updates is a new feature of Android 15, which enhances the platform's update process' adaptability and effectiveness. With this improvement, Google can update NFC components without updating the entire system, which speeds up the distribution of security updates and feature upgrades to NFC-capable devices.

Delivering important security patches to NFC-capable devices faster is one of the main benefits of severing the connection between NFC components and system upgrades.

Google can swiftly address security vulnerabilities in NFC components and lower the danger of hostile actors exploiting them by keeping NFC upgrades apart from complete system updates.

Furthermore, by separating NFC components from system updates, Google is able to add new NFC capabilities and improvements without needing to release a whole system update, hence improving the platform's flexibility and modularity. As a result, NFC functionality may be improved more frequently and specifically, giving users access to the newest features without having to wait for significant platform updates.

Moreover, the efficiency of the update process is increased by separating NFC components from system upgrades, which cuts down on the time and resources needed to distribute NFC updates to compatible devices. In addition to improving user experience overall and guaranteeing that customers may continue to enjoy dependable NFC capabilities on their Android devices, this simplifies the upkeep and support of NFC-enabled devices.

In general, the separation of NFC components from system updates in Android 15 is a noteworthy progress in the platform's update system. Android 15 enhances NFC-capable devices' security, adaptability, and efficiency by permitting separate upgrades for NFC components, so consumers may take advantage of dependable and safe NFC capabilities right now.

Finally, a variety of technological improvements are included in Android 15 with the goal of enhancing the platform's performance, security, and user experience. Android 15 is a major advancement in the growth of the Android operating system, featuring enhancements to file integrity, performance optimizations, built-in phishing protection, Bluetooth LE Audio support, and NFC decoupling. Google's dedication to providing a stable, secure, and intuitive platform that caters to the changing requirements of both users and developers is demonstrated by these improvements.

Chapter 6: Developer Insights

Developer Preview of Android 15

An early peek at future features, APIs, and modifications to the Android operating system is provided to developers through the Android 15 Developer Preview. Before the official release, it gives developers the chance to test their apps on the newest version of Android and make sure they work together.

Early access to new tools and APIs is one of the main advantages of the Developer

Preview, enabling developers to utilize the newest platform features and incorporate them into their projects. Developers can remain ahead of the curve and provide users with cutting-edge experiences thanks to this early access.

Moreover, the Developer Preview enables developers to inform Google of any problems or queries they run into while testing. This feedback loop is essential to enhancing the platform's performance and reliability prior to the final release, guaranteeing a seamless transition for consumers and developers alike.

All things considered, the Android 15 Developer Preview is a great tool for developers to get their apps ready for the upcoming Android release and help shape the platform's continued development.

Tools for Development and Testing

With Android 15, developers will have access to a new set of testing and development tools that will enable them to create high-caliber apps faster. To guarantee a flawless user experience, these tools expedite the development process, improve the quality of the code, and enable extensive testing.

The official integrated development environment (IDE) for creating Android apps, Android Studio, is one such tool. With Android Studio, developers can create, debug, and test apps with a robust toolkit that includes integrated emulators, sophisticated code analysis functions, and support for the most recent platform APIs.

Android 15 brings improvements to the Android Jetpack library, a set of tools and libraries created to speed up the creation of Android apps, in addition to Android Studio. Jetpack components like ViewModel, LiveData, and Navigation make basic development activities easier to do and make it easier for developers to create reliable, maintainable programs more quickly.

Additionally, Android 15 brings enhancements to the Android Testing Framework, which facilitate the creation and implementation of automated tests for developers' apps. New testing APIs, enhanced instrumentation testing capability, and interoperability with well-known testing frameworks like Espresso and JUnit are some of these improvements.

All things considered, Android 15's development and testing tools enable developers to create high-caliber apps faster, with less development time and better app performance and dependability.

Updates and Additions to the API

The Android platform APIs have undergone a number of modifications and additions with Android 15, giving developers more tools and capabilities to improve their apps. With the help of these API modifications, developers can create more robust, feature-rich apps that take advantage of recent platform developments.

The release of new APIs in Android 15 for managing partial screen sharing is one noteworthy update.

By giving developers the option to choose which app content to transmit during screen recording, this functionality enhances user privacy and usability. Now that particular apps may be designated for screen sharing, developers can make sure that private data is safe.

Furthermore, Android 15 brings improvements to the camera API that let developers boost the quality of photos and videos in apps that are used by third parties. With the help of new capabilities like enhanced brightness in low light and sophisticated flash strength changes, developers can provide consumers with superior photography experiences.

Additionally, Android 15 adds support for virtual MIDI 2.0 devices, enhancing the platform's potential for applications related to audio and music production. Android developers now have the ability to create virtual MIDI applications that operate synthesizer apps just like USB MIDI devices, creating new opportunities for Android music production.

All things considered, Android 15's API enhancements and modifications present developers with fascinating new chances to be creative and produce engaging, high-performing apps.

Developers can maintain their leadership position in Android app development and provide users with richer, more engaging experiences by utilizing these new APIs.

To sum up, Android 15's developer insights provide developers with an extensive array of tools, resources, and APIs to enable them to create high-caliber apps faster. With the Developer Preview offering early access, robust development and testing tools, and new and updated APIs, Android 15 gives developers the tools they need to build cutting-edge, feature-rich apps that push the limits of what is feasible on the Android platform.

Conclusion

Summary and Prospects

Finally, with a plethora of new features and improvements targeted at enhancing user experience, security, and performance, Android 15 marks a major turning point in the development of the Android operating system. The comprehensive set of changes offered by Android 15 promises to improve the Android experience for both developers and consumers. These improvements range from visual upgrades and new features to technological improvements and developer insights.

With its new logo and slogan, "Vanilla Ice Cream," Android 15's visual improvements give the platform a more contemporary appearance without sacrificing its recognizable Android style. Users across the platform will receive a unified and visually appealing experience thanks to these visual improvements and the space-themed design elements.

Android 15 brings with it a plethora of new features and updates aimed at boosting user security, privacy, and productivity. With features like improved screen sharing, improved camera performance, support for virtual MIDI 2.0 devices, and upgrades to the privacy sandbox, Android 15 offers a plethora of new capabilities that should improve Android for both consumers and developers.

With features like lock screen widgets, app pairing, simple mode, and the private space feature, Android 15's user experience has been improved. This gives users more customization options and flexibility to fit their own tastes and requirements with their devices. With these improvements, consumers now have greater control over their devices and improved usability and accessibility.

Android 15 brings a number of technical enhancements to improve device security, performance, and connectivity. With features like built-in phishing protection, Bluetooth LE Audio support, file integrity enhancements, and speed optimizations, Android 15 gives developers a wealth of tools to craft safe, fast apps that take advantage of the newest platform developments.

With Android 15, developers can create high-caliber apps more quickly and effectively thanks to enhancements and additions to the API, tools for testing and development, and the Developer Preview.

With the help of the Developer Preview, developers can prepare their apps for the upcoming Android version and continue to contribute to the platform's progress by getting early access to new features and APIs. Development and testing tools help developers produce dependable, high-performing apps for customers by streamlining the development process and facilitating comprehensive testing. Developers can create cutting-edge, feature-rich experiences that push the limits of what is possible on the Android platform with the help of API additions and updates, which provide them additional tools and capabilities to improve their apps.

Android looks to have a bright future ahead of it, with new releases likely to bring along even more innovation and advancement. Android will continue to lead mobile technology for many years to come thanks to Google's dedication to provide a stable, secure, and intuitive platform. The platform will expand further and offer new experiences and opportunities to both users and developers as long as users and developers accept the most recent features and capabilities added in Android 15. Android 15 lays the groundwork for a promising future for the Android ecosystem by prioritizing security, efficiency, and user experience.

www.ingramcontent.com/pod-product-compliance
Lightning Source LLC
Chambersburg PA
CBHW061049050326
40690CB00012B/2567